101

About

Taylor Swift

The Unofficial Kid and Teen Quiz & Trivia Guide to the Amazing Popstar

Luna Jones

WELCOME TO EVERYTHING TAYLOR SWIFT

Welcome to the Taylor Swift Trivia Book-101 Intriguing Facts and 80 Questions To Test Your Knowledge Of Taylor Swift! This book gives an in-depth examination of Taylor Swift; her life, her achievements and her rise to becoming a pivotal figure in contemporary music and pop culture. Within this book, we'll delve into the exceptional talent, hard work and influence of Taylor, who has persistently raised the bar in the music industry and has become a beacon of inspiration and creativity for fans worldwide.

This collection of pages contains a thoughtfully curated selection of facts, stories and pivotal moments that trace every step of Taylor Swift's journey-from her humble origins in Reading, Pennsylvania to her current status as a worldwide music sensation and cultural icon. Each fact has been extensively researched and presented in a way that provides a comprehensive understanding of Taylor's lasting influence-and not just in the music industry!

So let's get ready to delve into the fascinating world of Taylor Swift with this exciting book!

The book is divided into two main parts designed to inform and entertain readers of all ages.

The first section, called '101 Facts about Taylor,' takes you on a journey through the personal and professional life of Taylor Swift-showcasing her accomplishments and contributions to the music world and societal issues in a unique and randomized fashion!

The second half, the 'Trivia/Quiz' section, is packed with a range of questions to test your Taylor Swift knowledge-from straightforward everyday facts to more head scratching about Taylor's life and career. Whether you're a die-hard Taylor Swift fan or just looking for a fun and informative read, this book is the perfect choice!

101 Facts About Taylor

1.   Taylor Swift was born on a chilly winter's day-December 13, 1989-which might explain why her songs often carry the crisp whisper of winter. As a Sagittarius born in the heart of the cold season, Taylor's music draws inspiration from frosty landscapes and silent, snowy nights, weaving these elements into magical melodies and heartwarming lyrics. Her birthday, when nature is draped in a serene white blanket, has subtly influenced her songwriting, allowing her to capture the essence of winter's enchantment in her tunes.

2.   Since she was young, Taylor Swift dreamed of becoming a Broadway star. Despite growing up in a small town, her aspirations never wavered. She often traveled to New York City, the entertainment hub of the world, to learn everything she could about music and acting. During these trips Taylor absorbed all the knowledge she could, honing her singing and performing skills. These experiences in the big city helped her become the superstar she is today, teaching her how to engage with her audience and convey stories through her songs-just like a true Broadway performer!

DID YOU KNOW?

3.   When Taylor Swift got her first 12-string guitar, it changed everything. This unique instrument was more than just a tool for music; it became her best friend, helping her write amazing songs by bringing her feelings and ideas to life. With each strum, she felt like she could create something extraordinary- and she did! Her guitar helped her produce songs that people all over the world could relate to and love. Thanks to her 12-string guitar, Taylor Swift became a famous musician whose music has touched the hearts of many.

4.   At just 12 years old, Taylor wrote her first song, 'Lucky You.' This song was not only a playful experiment, but it also showcased her early talent for weaving emotions into words. Even at such a young age, Taylor could capture complex feelings in simple lyrics, which set the stage for her future as a masterful songwriter. This was the beginning of her incredible journey in music, where her talent for crafting stories through song has touched the hearts of people worldwide.

DID YOU KNOW?

5.   Taylor Swift's music is a beautiful combination of country vibes and opera grandeur-attributed to her grandmother, an opera singer. This influence from a young age allowed Taylor to combine opera's emotionally intense tunes with country storytelling in her music, with this unique blend playing a significant role in shaping Taylor's distinctive sound. Being heavily influenced by both musical styles in her childhood, she began her journey in the country genre, successfully merging both worlds and crafting songs that narrate stories with elegance and musical beauty.

6.   When she was only 14 years old, Taylor Swift's family made a big decision to move to Nashville, the hub of country music, due to her unwavering dedication and blossoming talent. This move was more than just a relocation; it was a turning point in Taylor's musical journey. Taylor discovered her true calling in Nashville, a city with musical possibilities and alive with rhythm. The dynamic city, renowned for its rich musical heritage, provided a nurturing environment where she honed her skills and turned her dreams into reality, paving the way for her rise in the music industry.

DID YOU KNOW?

7.   As a teenager, the music world was abuzz when Taylor became the youngest ever writer/artist to sign a deal with Sony/ATV Tree publishing house in Nashville. This wasn't just any old record deal; it was a clear indication of her prodigious talent and a sign of her future success. At such a young age, securing a place in Nashville's music scene was no easy feat-it was an extraordinary achievement that demonstrated her potential and hinted at the legendary career to come. Taylor's early entry into the industry was impressive, promising a spectacular musical journey.

8.   In 2006, Taylor Swift released her debut album, the self-titled 'Taylor Swift.' The album was a significant moment in music history, marking the beginning of her career and showcasing her unique storytelling and musical style. It was not just a collection of tracks, but a declaration of her arrival onto the global music platform and a cultural phenomenon that would reshape the music landscape for generations to come. 'Taylor Swift' was a huge triumph that established her as a rising star in the country music scene and set the stage for a revolutionary career.

DID YOU KNOW?

9.   Even as Taylor Swift rose to fame, she did not neglect her studies. With her music career flourishing, she stayed committed to her homeschooling. She effortlessly balanced her academic and musical pursuits, demonstrating her strong belief in nurturing her mind and creative abilities. Taylor's dedication to education and art shows she understands that personal growth and artistic expression are equally essential.

10.   Taylor Swift's album 'Fearless' was released in 2008 and was a game-changer in showcasing her growing musical prowess. This album was a hit and a Grammy magnet-winning four of these coveted music industry awards, including the top honor of Album of the Year. Taylor was the youngest to clinch this prize at the time, proving her extraordinary talent and securing her position as a music industry powerhouse. 'Fearless' was more than just an album; it was a statement of Taylor's artistic ability and a preview of her remarkable career path.

DID YOU KNOW?

11.   Taylor Swift isn't just a singing sensation; she also made a splash in the acting world! She lit up the screen in the romantic comedy 'Valentine's Day' in 2010, charming everyone as a bubbly high school student. But that's not all-Taylor also lent her voice to the animated movie 'The Lorax' from 2012, bringing the character Audrey to life. These acting gigs showed her fans a new aspect of her talent, proving that Taylor's creativity knows no bounds and highlighting her flair for both music and acting.

12.   Not only is she an incredible musician, but she's also an incredibly kind and generous person. Taylor has a big heart, and she uses her fame to positively impact the world in a multitude of ways. She's involved in many humanitarian endeavors, from supporting education and disaster relief to advocating for the LGBTQ+ community. Her actions show she truly cares about making a difference and spreading hope-she's not just a music icon, but also an inspiration to many.

DID YOU KNOW?

13.   In 2014, Taylor Swift demonstrated immense courage by challenging Spotify about the compensation of artists. She not only sang about change but also took bold action to bring attention to the treatment and payment of musicians in the age of streaming. Her inspiring move sparked worldwide conversations about the rights of artists and the true worth of their music in the digital era. Taylor's stance was not just for her music, but for all artists, ensuring that their creative work was valued and rewarded fairly.

14.   In 2014, Taylor Swift released her album '1989,' which marked a turning point in her career by transitioning from country to pop music. The album was an instant hit, featuring lively synth-pop tracks that earned her a Grammy Award for Album of the Year. What made this album significant was that it showcased Swift's versatility in music, proving her ability to excel in any genre. '1989' was more than just a collection of catchy tunes-it was a bold and daring move that demonstrated Swift's capacity to succeed in the fast-paced, constantly changing world of pop music.

DID YOU KNOW?

15.   A vocal supporter of artistic integrity, Taylor has been fighting tirelessly to help artists retain control over their own music. Her recent battle to reclaim her master recordings has brought to the forefront the challenges that artists often face in the music industry. Taylor is not just fighting for herself; she is fighting for all musicians to have the freedom to own their creations. Taylor has become a leading figure in the quest for fairness in the music industry and has earned deep respect from both her fans and fellow musicians.

16.   Did you know that Taylor Swift's album 'Red' is like a colorful musical puzzle? It was released in 2012 and is filled with songs that tell stories about growing up and experiencing various emotions. Taylor mixed different music styles in 'Red,' just like an artist uses many colors to paint a picture. She showed us that trying new things and being bold with our creativity can be enjoyable. 'Red' is not just an album, it's a journey through Taylor's adventures in music-where every song is a piece of her heart!

DID YOU KNOW?

17.   Taylor Swift hit a milestone when she was 19, winning her first MTV Video Music Award (VMA) for 'You Belong With Me.' Her 2009 victory was more than just a win-it highlighted her emerging prominence in music. Winning a VMA early on spotlighted her talent and set the stage for future triumphs, making her a notable pop and country music figure. This accolade was the first of many, as Taylor captivated both audiences and critics with her musical talent and narrative ability.

18.   At that same 2009 MTV Video Music Awards show, Kanye West interrupted Taylor Swift's acceptance speech for Best Female Video, claiming Beyoncé's video was one of the best of all time. This sparked public discourse on respect and sportsmanship in the entertainment industry. Despite the awkward situation, Taylor handled it gracefully and professionally, earning further admiration from the public and her fans. This marked a significant moment in pop culture history, and is possibly one of the most memorable incidents from an award show in decades!

DID YOU KNOW?

19. Taylor Swift's track 'Out of the Woods' succeeded remarkably, breaking records by staying at Number 1 on the charts for six consecutive weeks. Released as part of her critically acclaimed album '1989,' this song captivated listeners worldwide with its catchy melody and emotionally resonant lyrics, reflecting Taylor's journey and challenges in the spotlight. The song's endurance at the top of the charts is a testament to its widespread appeal and Taylor's skill as a songwriter and artist. This achievement highlighted both the song's popularity and Taylor Swift's impact on the industry.

20. Amazingly, Taylor Swift has won the Nashville Songwriters Association's Songwriter-Artist of the Year award not once, not twice-but seven times! With a songwriting technique that borders on magic, Taylor continues to touch hearts all around the world with the stories woven into her music. Her songs are veritable treasure troves of emotion, each contributing to making her one of the brightest stars in songwriting.

DID YOU KNOW?

21.   Taylor Swift's 'Eras Tour' is an epic showcase of her musical journey, featuring an astonishing number of individual shows spanning dozens of countries across the globe. With 152 scheduled concerts, Taylor is setting the stage alight for nearly 495 hours throughout this tour-that's over 20 days of live performance! This record-breaking tour not only highlights her enduring popularity but also her incredible stamina and dedication to her fans-making it a monumental chapter in her career and cementing her place in music history.

22.   On the topic of live performances, her reputation for electrifying shows has been well-established through her previous tours. During the '1989 World Tour' in 2015, she performed 85 shows, amounting to approximately 255 hours of stage time, while her later 'Reputation Stadium Tour' in 2018 included 53 shows, translating to around 159 hours of live performance. Before these, the 'Red Tour' spanning 2013 to 2014 saw her on stage for 86 shows-about 258 hours. The tours, totaling over 672 hours of live music, showed Taylor's commitment to her fans and showcasing her musical versatility.

DID YOU KNOW?

23.   In 2013, Taylor Swift demonstrated that she held music education close to her heart, donating a generous $4 million to the Country Music Hall of Fame and Museum and leading to the subsequent creation of the 'Taylor Swift Education Center.' Taylor's contribution highlights her commitment to helping young musicians learn and grow, and her support ensures that the music industry continues to thrive with both fresh talent and passion.

24.   Making history at the American Music Awards, Taylor Swift now holds the record for the most award wins ever as a female artist, underscoring her lasting appeal and impact in the music world. This impressive feat-not to mention her growing collection of AMAs-showcases her as a leading figure in her era, widely celebrated and honored for her musical talents and achievements.

DID YOU KNOW?

25.   Taylor Swift took fan interaction to an almost unbelievable level with her '1989 Secret Sessions'- during this event, several lucky fans were invited to Taylor's own home to receive a sneak peek of her new album before anyone else in the world! Beyond merely an industry preview, these intimate gatherings weren't just about listening to her music; they were magical moments where Taylor glimpsed her world, making her fans feel like they were part of her inner circle.

26.   Not to be satisfied with music superstardom alone, Taylor Swift is also a real estate expert! With eight properties totaling over $81 million, she has impressive homes in a wide variety of places, including Nashville, New York City, Rhode Island, and Los Angeles. Each of these homes isn't just a place to stay-they're a wise investment, showing off Taylor's savvy business acumen and knack for picking the perfect spots to call home, from country havens to city penthouses.

27.   For all her fearless performances, Taylor has a rather unusual phobia: sea urchins! She's gone on record describing these ocean dwellers as "lurking predators," with the spiny little spheres making the sea all the more scary for her. It's a surprising fear for someone who seems unstoppable on stage, reminding us that even larger-than-life icons like Taylor have their own unique phobias, just like the rest of us.

28.   On the other hand, Taylor Swift is a huge cat lover! Her home is alive with the sounds of scampering paws from the several adorable cats she shares her house with. Each of her furry friends has a unique personality, all holding a special place in her heart. Taylor loves sharing cute photos and funny stories of her cats on social media, making her fans fawn over the charming felines every time. From celebrating their birthdays to capturing their silly moments, Taylor's bond with her cats is genuine and heartwarming.

29.   At the sprightly age of 12, Taylor wasn't only dreaming about music-she was already an author in the making! Penning an impressive 350-page novel in her youth, the story is a testament to her creativity blossoming early in life. While this novel never made it to bookstore shelves, it clearly indicates Taylor's artistic flair extending beyond melodies and lyrics to the written word. This early achievement highlights her innate talent and the multitude of ways she expresses her creativity, showcasing that her storytelling skills were just as sharp as her songwriting ones from the start.

30.   Taylor Swift loves the outdoors, finding a unique kind of inspiration tucked away in the quiet corners of nature. But it's not just about enjoying the scenery-it's a vital part of her creative process. Hiking through peaceful forests and spending time under the open sky, she connects with a world of quiet tranquility far removed from the spotlight. This connection with nature provides a relaxing hobby and a chance for nature's creativity to subtly weave its way into her music, helping to spark the ideas for her following chart-topping songs.

DID YOU KNOW?

31.   Taylor's has a passion for collecting snow globes! With a collection numbering over a hundred globes, she has curated a fascinating array of these enchanting objects that is more than just a hobby-it's an obsession! Each snow globe in her collection encapsulates a unique story or memory that is dear to her, making them among her favorite possessions. It's no surprise that her snow globe collection is a reflection of her creativity, imagination, and love for the art of storytelling.

32.   Taylor Swift isn't just about catchy tunes and vocals-she's also skilled with a variety of different instruments. Besides strumming the guitar, she can tickle the ivories on the piano, pluck the strings of a banjo, and strum the ukulele. Taylor has a knack for music beyond just singing; she can make melodies come to life in many ways, and her instrumental skills showcase how talented a musician she truly is.

DID YOU KNOW?

33.   Taylor shares a heartwarming sibling bond that goes beyond mere family ties. Growing up together, they developed a deep connection that has stood the test of both time and fame. This strong relationship is often mirrored in Taylor's lyrics, where she occasionally hints at Austin's supportive and grounding presence in her life. Their closeness can be heard through her songs. As an actor, Austin has his own creative pursuits-yet he and Taylor remain closely knit, highlighting the importance of family in Taylor's personal and professional journey.

34.   Taylor Swift spent her early years growing up on a Christmas tree farm in Pennsylvania. This experience shaped her down-to-earth personality and work ethic. This setting, with its endless rows of bristling pine trees, provided a magical backdrop for her childhood, instilling a love for nature and the simple joys of life. Growing up on the farm, Taylor was involved in the family business, quickly learning the value of hard work in the countryside. It helped to inspire many of the storytelling elements she would go on to use in her music.

DID YOU KNOW?

35. Taylor Swift's journey from battling stage fright to owning the spotlight shows that great things can start with small steps. As a child, she felt nervous before performances but didn't let fear stop her. Instead, she faced it head-on, performing at local events and talent shows. Each performance built her confidence and skill, transforming her into the global superstar she is today. Taylor's story teaches us that with determination, passion, and courage, we can turn our dreams into reality, no matter how daunting they seem.

36. Taylor Swift's song "Fifteen" feels like a letter to our younger selves, especially with the line, "But in your life, you'll do things greater than dating the boy on the football team." She reminds kids that high school drama isn't everything and that exciting things lie ahead. Growing up can be tough, but Taylor's song encourages young people to look forward to the future and the many dreams they have yet to chase.

DID YOU KNOW?

37.   In her catchy song 'Shake It Off,' Taylor sings about continuing no matter what, with the words, "But I keep cruising, can't stop, won't stop moving." In her own way, she's telling her fans that sometimes it's okay not to dwell on the bad moments in life and just dance it off, as if saying to listeners, "Don't worry about the small things; keep smiling and moving forward." This song is like a fun, musical reminder that we can all shake off our worries and enjoy life to the fullest.

38.   The lyric "Just because you're clean don't mean you don't miss it" from her song 'Clean' is a powerful message of hope and resilience. It reminds us that overcoming challenges doesn't mean forgetting the past or the hardships we've faced-instead, it's about growing stronger and moving forward while recognizing the struggles we've endured and the lessons we've learned from them. This line encourages fans to find strength in their journey and to see that moving past difficulties is a testament to their resilience, offering a beacon of hope to those navigating their own challenges.

DID YOU KNOW?

39.   Similarly, Taylor's song 'The Man' talks about being yourself and not letting expectations of who you should be slow down. She sings, "I'm so sick of running as fast as I can, wondering if I'd get there quicker if I was a man," telling everyone-especially young kids-that it's okay to question why things are the way they are. Taylor encourages us to dream big and fight for what we believe in, whether we're a boy or a girl. She wants us to know that everyone deserves the chance to reach for their dreams, showing us that being strong is for everyone.

40.   Taylor's 2009 to 2010 'Fearless' tour was a huge blockbuster, raking in over $63 million and drawing fans from across the globe. Showcasing her as a live music sensation, this tour featured songs from her 'Fearless' album and demonstrated her exceptional ability to connect with the audience, solidifying her reputation as a leading concert performer and setting new standards for live country-pop music shows. The tour's success marked a significant milestone in Taylor's career, establishing her as a major concert draw and paving the way for her future sold-out tours.

DID YOU KNOW?

41. In the 'Miss Americana' documentary, Taylor Swift shared a surprising personal detail about her life: she tasted her first burrito at 26. This revelation offers a glimpse into the life of the globally renowned music artist known for her relatable songwriting and grounded persona. The documentary provides a behind-the-scenes look at her life and career, highlighting little moments like this that showcase Taylor's willingness to try new things-even in her everyday life.

42. Taylor Swift's family has a particularly unique member-a support dog named Kitty, who played a crucial role during her mom Andrea's battle with cancer. More than a pet, Kitty served as a comforting companion and source of strength for Andrea during her treatment and recovery. This support dog's presence underscored the healing power of animal companionship and the deep bond shared between the Swift family and their pets, reflecting the care and love that helped them through challenging times.

DID YOU KNOW?

43. At 16, Taylor Swift embraced the typical teenage milestone of learning to drive, which marked her transition toward independence. This experience-set against her early life in Pennsylvania-was not just about getting behind the wheel; it symbolized her journey toward self-reliance and maturity. Learning to drive gave Taylor a taste of freedom and responsibility, reflecting her down-to-earth upbringing and foreshadowing the determination and autonomy she would later bring to her music career.

44. Talking about Sweet 16, Taylor Swift has a special place in her heart for cheesecake, which she counts among her favorite indulgences. This preference for the creamy, decadent dessert adds a relatable and personal dimension to her superstar persona, revealing her penchant for classic comforts. Cheesecake, with its rich flavor and smooth texture, resonates with Taylor's taste buds, offering a glimpse into the simple joys she cherishes. This tidbit both connects Taylor with her fans over shared food favorites and highlights her appreciation for life's sweeter moments.

DID YOU KNOW?

45.   When Taylor Swift was growing up, she became friends with Abigail Anderson, with the two of them sharing many experiences that have deeply inspired Taylor's songwriting over the years. Abigail's powerful influence on Taylor's life is reflected in her music-in fact, Taylor's song 'Fifteen,' which is part of her 'Fearless' album, captures the depth of their friendship. In the song, Taylor talks about their high school experiences and how Abigail gave everything she had to a boy who changed his mind.

46.   Guess what? Taylor Swift is not just a singer; she's a songwriter superhero, too! In 2010, the Songwriters Hall of Fame awarded Taylor and brought her into their ranks, showing their appreciation of her incredible writing talent-a feat that only a few other artists can claim! Taylor's songs are like magic spells-she uses her words to create feelings and stories that we can sing along to and feel in our hearts. Like a storybook hero, Taylor uses her pen to take us on wonderful adventures with her songs and lyrics!

DID YOU KNOW?

47.   Did you know Taylor Swift has her own line of perfumes? That's right! She created fragrances like 'Wonderstruck' and 'Enchanted' to let fans experience her art in a whole new way-through smell! These perfumes are like a touch of her own musical magic in a bottle, bringing the sweet and sparkly vibes of her songs into a scent you can wear. So, with a spritz of her perfume, you can carry a piece of Taylor's world with you all day!

48.   Taylor is a world-renowned musician and a passionate learner who believes everyone should have access to education. She generously donates books and funds to schools and libraries so that children can read and learn in both fun and engaging ways. Taylor's belief in the power of education is so strong that she goes out of her way to help communities grow smarter and stronger-her contributions have helped many children discover the joy of learning and positively impacted their lives. It is truly inspiring to see how Taylor uses her music stardom for the greater good !

DID YOU KNOW?

49. Taylor Swift is a record-breaking superstar! Not just famous for her catchy songs, she's also a champion in setting world records. Can you believe she has a spot in the Guinness World Records? One of her most popular records is for having the fastest-selling digital album by a female artist- that's a lot of people worldwide who wanted to listen to her music the second it came out! Taylor is an extraordinary achiever in the music industry, leading the way with her amazing tunes and record- setting achievements-she's like the queen of pop music, constantly surprising us with her talents!

50. Did you hear about Taylor Swift's amazing musical adventure 'Speak Now?' In 2010, she did something incredible: she wrote every song on that album by herself! That's right, from the first note to the last lyric, it was all Taylor's work, showing off her incredible songwriting skills. 'Speak Now' is like a diary filled with Taylor's thoughts and stories, turned into catchy tunes that everyone can enjoy. This album isn't just music-it's a peek into Taylor's world, crafted lovingly with her hands, heart and voice, making it a unique gem in her hits collection!

DID YOU KNOW?

51.　The '1989 World Tour' was an epic celebration of Taylor Swift's music that rocked the entire world. It wasn't just any ordinary concert series-it was a massive party that showcased her talent and made her one of the top money-making performers of the decade. People from all over the globe eagerly awaited the opportunity to witness Taylor's live performances, proving that she's an incredible singer and a superstar on stage. The '1989' tour showcased her talent, illuminating entire cities with her hit songs and breathtaking performances.

52.　Taylor Swift shines as a beacon for equality, championing women's rights and inspiring fans with her commitment to gender fairness. Beyond her catchy tunes, she's a vocal advocate for treating everyone equally, leveraging her fame to challenge and shine a spotlight on injustices. Her actions and words resonate worldwide, transforming her into a modern symbol of feminism. Taylor's journey from pop star to empowered advocate illustrates her deep belief in equality, making her a role model and a voice for positive societal change.

DID YOU KNOW?

53.   You probably know by now that she writes her own songs, but guess who's also a superstar in both singing and directing her own music videos? That's right-Taylor Swift! Taylor set another milestone in her career by becoming the first woman to win the MTV Video Music Award for Video of the Year for a video she directed herself-meaning she not only sang the song, but also decided how the video should look. Like being a band's producer and lead singer at the same time, Taylor shows us that you can be super talented in more than one way-and she's continuing to lead the charge with her awesome music videos!

54.   Do you know what's impressive about Taylor Swift? When she dropped her self-titled first album, she had written or co-written every single song on it-and you know what? The album went on to receive a platinum certification and became hugely popular! This made her the first-ever female country singer to achieve this with her debut album-like being the first person to reach the summit of a mountain! Taylor Swift is an incredibly talented artist who started with a bang by showcasing her exceptional skills in her debut album through her words and tunes.

DID YOU KNOW?

55.   Taylor Swift decided to take a break from the spotlight after becoming a hot topic on Twitter, where the media attention was intense and caused her to trend globally. She felt it was essential to step back and take some time for herself to escape the public eye and media scrutiny. This break helped her find peace away from the constant buzz and talk online, allowing her to focus on her well-being and creativity.

56.   Can you believe that some people have actually proposed to their loved ones at a Taylor Swift concert, with Taylor herself as part of their special moment? It's true! While the exact number of happy couples isn't known, these romantic proposals have become a unique part of her concerts. Imagine popping the question with one of the biggest music stars as your witness, creating a magical and unforgettable proposal story!

DID YOU KNOW?

57.   Taylor Swift's houses have attracted some unwelcome visitors. There have been a few instances where people have broken into her homes-one unwanted guest even took a nap in her bed! This is not only scary but also a big invasion of privacy, highlighting the many challenges that come with fame. It shows that even famous people like Taylor can face unexpected situations at home, emphasizing the need for strong security measures.

58.   Taylor Swift has flown in several private jets over the years, using them to travel to concerts, events and vacations, showing the high-flying lifestyle that comes with her global fame. Traveling the world in over 20 different jets, it's known that she prefers this way of travel for comfort and privacy. These jets help her reach her fans all over the world, manage her busy schedule and keep a level of personal space away from the public eye.

DID YOU KNOW?

59. As for owning private jets, Taylor Swift has had a few to call her own, reflecting her success and need for convenient, private travel. At one point, she owned two private jets, allowing her to fly wherever she needed-whether for tours, recording sessions or just a quick getaway-providing her with the ultimate travel flexibility and luxury.

60. 'ME!' by Taylor Swift, featuring Brendon Urie, is like a magical journey into Taylor's imagination-a place where bright colors and joy swirl around every corner. She's described the song as a reflection of the kaleidoscope of thoughts and fantasies dancing in her mind. This track expresses her vibrant personality and artistic flair, filled with catchy tunes and playful lyrics that bring to life the enchanting and whimsical world she envisions. It's like opening the door to a fun-filled realm where Taylor's creativity knows no bounds, inviting listeners to join in the celebration.

DID YOU KNOW?

61.   Taylor Swift loves cars and has a few in her collection, enjoying the freedom and style that come with driving different models. Owning a total of 5-6 cars-including a Ferrari 458 and a Porsche 911 Turbo-she has been seen in various stylish cars over the years. Each one in her garage reflects a part of her personality-from classic to modern and chic, showing her taste in music and automobiles.

62.   Taylor Swift has a wide collection of homes across the United States, ranging from the musical heart of Nashville to the bustling streets of New York City and the sun-kissed hills of Beverly Hills. Each home mirrors her personal taste, blending elegance with comfort and serving as a sanctuary where she can unwind, find inspiration and craft her next musical masterpiece. They symbolize her journey from a country singer to an international pop sensation, providing serene havens to nurture her talent and creativity in peace.

DID YOU KNOW?

63.   The Swift family's home in Nashville, Tennessee, is more than just a house-it's a foundation stone in Taylor Swift's musical odyssey. Her parents moved there to nurture her talent, a decision that proved pivotal in her rise to stardom. This home witnessed Taylor's transformation from a hopeful young artist to a global superstar, imbued with memories of her early steps in music. Nestled in the city that sparked her meteoric rise, the Swift family home is a heartfelt emblem of their unwavering support and belief in Taylor's dreams.

64.   Taylor Swift's music has dominated the charts over the years since her debut, spending over 150 weeks at number one and showcasing her massive success and popularity. With numerous hit songs and albums, Taylor has broken records and set new benchmarks in the music industry, proving her enduring appeal and strong connection with fans worldwide. Her chart-topping streaks reflect her ability to consistently produce beloved and catchy tunes that resonate with listeners, cementing her status as a music icon.

DID YOU KNOW?

65.   Taylor Swift has worked with various producers throughout her career-but one of her most notable collaborators is Jack Antonoff. Antonoff has been a critical figure in the production of several of Swift's albums, including '1989,' 'Reputation,' 'Lover,' 'Folklore' and 'Evermore,' helping to shape the sound and style of her music. Their partnership has resulted in some of Swift's most critically acclaimed and commercially successful work, highlighting a creative synergy that has significantly influenced her musical direction.

66.   The inspiration behind Taylor Swift's song 'The Man' comes from her reflections on gender double standards and the different societal expectations that men and women face. In this song, she imagines how her career and public image might have been perceived differently if she were a man, addressing issues of inequality and sexism. 'The Man' is a powerful commentary on women's challenges-particularly in the entertainment industry-and has resonated with listeners for its candid and thought-provoking lyrics.

DID YOU KNOW?

67. Taylor Swift's journey through her political beliefs has shifted from being quiet to vocal; advocating for women's rights, LGBTQ+ equality and racial justice. Her political awakening shone brightly during the 2018 U.S. midterm elections, where she endorsed democratic candidates and urged her fans to vote, demonstrating her commitment to making a difference. This move had a significant impact, reportedly inspiring a surge in young voter registrations.

68. With a massive following on Instagram, Taylor Swift has over 280 million followers. Her Instagram account is a window into her life, career and interests-with over 600 posts allowing her to connect with fans personally. Swift's dominating presence on social media is a testament to her popularity and the strong bond she shares with her audience, all of whom are drawn to her authenticity and relatability.

DID YOU KNOW?

69.   Taylor Swift's 'Reputation Stadium Tour' was notable for its extensive outfit changes, showcasing her sense of style and the theatrical nature of her performances. Each concert featured 16 costume changes-ranging from glamorous dresses to edgy ensembles and complementing her songs' different themes and moods. The tour was a fashion spectacle as much as a musical one, with Swift's wardrobe changes adding an extra layer of excitement and visual appeal to the already dynamic show.

70.   The 'Miss Americana' documentary showcases Taylor Swift's musical journey with more than 20 chart-topping hits playing in the background. Each song adds to her life and career narrative, from the upbeat 'Shake It Off' to the emotional 'All Too Well.' The film takes you on a musical expedition to reveal the layers of Taylor's artistry, with each track resonating with different chapters of her life. This cinematic playlist entertains and strengthens the connection between Taylor and her fans, making the documentary a symphony of her career's greatest moments.

DID YOU KNOW?

71. In the conclusion of 'Miss Americana,' Taylor Swift's song 'Only The Young' encapsulates the film's message of hope and action. The song is not just a concluding note but a powerful call to the younger generation, motivating them to rise, speak out and be the change in a world full of challenges. It captures the spirit of empowerment, change and the relentless pursuit of making one's voice count that is evident throughout the documentary.

72. 'Miss Americana' also delves into Taylor's personal struggles with body image and how the media's perception of her has affected her mental well-being. She talks candidly about her immense pressure to appear perfect in the public eye and the industry's unrealistic standards. By sharing her experiences, Taylor's vulnerability highlights the broader issues of body image and media influence, resonating with viewers who face similar challenges. Her honesty adds depth to the documentary and amplifies her role as an advocate for self-acceptance and mental health awareness.

DID YOU KNOW?

73.   Did you know Taylor Swift was a talented poet even before she became famous for her songs? As a fourth grader, she won a national poetry contest with her creative piece, 'Monster In My Closet.' This wasn't just a childhood achievement, but the start of Taylor's journey in crafting beautiful stories. Her early success in poetry showed that she had a special gift for words, paving the way for her future as a music superstar known for her captivating lyrics and storytelling magic.

74.   It's no secret that Taylor Swift is a highly sought-after figure for big brands looking to associate themselves with her glamorous lifestyle. Thanks to the backing of heavyweight sponsors like AT&T, Diet Coke and Apple Music, Taylor has taken her concerts to the next level, turning them into spectacular events. These sponsors not only provide financial support, but also play a crucial role in ensuring the smooth execution of her shows- helping her connect with fans all around the world.

DID YOU KNOW?

75.   Taylor Swift thought up her song 'Tim McGraw' in a place you might not expect-a math class! While sitting in school, instead of focusing on numbers and equations, Taylor's mind drifted to music-and that's where the magic happened. She crafted the idea for this song, blending her teenage experiences with her love of country music-all while she was supposed to be learning math!

76.   At the 2009 MTV Video Music Awards, Taylor Swift turned heads and captured hearts with her storybook entrance, arriving in a white horse-drawn carriage. This choice was a statement echoing the fairy-tale themes often found in her songs. As the carriage fit for a princess rolled up to the red carpet, it set the perfect scene for the evening, showcasing Taylor's love for blending fantasy with reality. This enchanting arrival highlighted her unique style and left an unforgettable mark on the history of the awards, illustrating Taylor's knack for creating magical, standout moments.

DID YOU KNOW?

77.   Taylor Swift is a world-renowned superstar, recognized multiple times as one of Time magazine's 100 most influential people. This highlights her far-reaching impact, which extends beyond her music to touch lives globally. Taylor's unique ability to connect with and inspire people from various cultures and backgrounds showcases her as an authentic global influencer, making her much more than simply a music icon. Her inclusion in the Time 100 list underscores her significant role in shaping the music industry and the broader cultural landscape.

78.   As you probably know, Taylor Swift has re-recorded some of her famous albums. She made new recordings of 'Fearless,' 'Red,' 'Speak Now,' and '1989,' calling them 'Taylor's Versions.' Taylor did this to have complete control of her music, making sure it was all hers. It took many months of hard work to re-record each album-but she did all of them with love and care. These unique versions let us hear her classic hits in a brand new way, showing how talented and determined Taylor is to share her music with the world in her own way!

DID YOU KNOW?

79.   Taylor has acted in 6 movies as both a voice and physical actor. Her acting resume includes films like 'Valentine's Day' (2010), 'The Lorax' (2012), 'The Giver' (2014), and 'Cats' (2019), and she also directed 'All Too Well: The Short Film' (2021) and 'Amsterdam' (2022). Taylor has also shared her musical journey through a multitude of documentary and concert films, including 'Journey to Fearless,' 'Speak Now World Tour – Live,' 'The 1989 World Tour Live,' 'Reputation Stadium Tour,' 'Miss Americana,' 'City of Lover,' 'Folklore: Long Pond Studio Sessions,' of which she also directed, and most recently 'The Eras Tour.'

80.   'Teardrops on My Guitar' was the second song that Taylor Swift ever released. It dropped on February 24, 2007 and quickly became a favorite, reaching No. 2 on the country charts and No. 33 on the pop charts. After its pop remix was released it soared even higher, reaching as high as No. 11 on numerous pop music lists. In October 2007, Taylor became the youngest artist ever to win the Songwriter/Artist of the Year award from the Nashville Songwriters Association International, pretty impressive for just her second song, don't you think?

DID YOU KNOW?

81.   Taylor didn't stop there; her third song, 'Our Song,' became a country music sensation, topping the charts for six weeks! Not only a hit in the country music world, it also reached No. 16 on the Billboard Hot 100 and No. 24 on the Pop 100. In 2007, Taylor shared her festive spirit with 'Sounds of the Season: The Taylor Swift Holiday Collection,' exclusively sold at Target. Although nominated for the Best New Artist Grammy in 2008, the award went to Amy Winehouse. Taylor's fourth single, 'Picture to Burn,' also from her debut album, soared to No. 3 on the Billboard Country chart in spring 2008.

82.   Swift made history on November 11, 2009, becoming the youngest artist to win the Entertainer of the Year award at the Country Music Association Awards-a feat only six other women have ever achieved! That same month, Taylor rocked the music world by simultaneously having eight of her songs on the Billboard Hot 100, a record for female artists. This happened when she re-released her album 'Fearless' and introduced five new songs that soared into the top 30, including 'Jump Then Fall' at number 10 and 'Untouchable' at number 19.

DID YOU KNOW?

83. In August 2017, Taylor Swift won a court case against David Mueller, a former radio DJ from Denver's KYGO-FM. Taylor had reported to Mueller's employers that he groped her at an event four years earlier. After Mueller lost his job, he claimed Taylor was lying and sued her for causing his unemployment. Taylor fought back by suing Mueller for sexual assault. Ultimately, the jury sided with Taylor, dismissing Mueller's accusations.

84. Before the '1989' album came out, Taylor emphasized the importance of albums for artists and fans. In November 2014, she removed her music from Spotify, citing unfair payment to songwriters. In June 2015, Taylor wrote a letter criticizing Apple Music for not paying artists during free trials. This led her to register 73 trademarks related to herself and the '1989' era. In June 2017, she returned her music to Spotify and other streaming platforms.

DID YOU KNOW?

85.   Taylor's electrifying and record-breaking 'The Eras Tour' kicked off with a bang on March 17, 2023 in Glendale, Arizona, and has been a whirlwind journey across five continents, spanning over 152 shows. The most epic concert tour in music history is scheduled to wrap up on December 8, 2024 in Vancouver, Canada. And the best part? 'The Eras Tour' has shattered all financial records-making over $1 billion in revenue, it's officially the highest-grossing concert tour ever witnessed. Hopefully you get the chance to see Taylor's incredible show live in action; if not, there's always the option of streaming!

86.   Taylor Swift's Eras Tour has captivated fans across the globe, creating a frenzied demand for tickets. In Lisbon, Portugal, tickets were snapped up within 2.5 hours of going on sale, while in Madrid, Spain, the overwhelming demand led to an additional show being scheduled, showcasing Swift's immense popularity. Japan experienced such intense interest that organizers held a second lottery for ticket sales. In Argentina, about one million fans rushed to secure the 24,000 available presale tickets, soaring to over three million for the general sale.

DID YOU KNOW?

87. In the United States, Taylor Swift's Eras Tour became a phenomenal spectacle in the music industry, demonstrating an extraordinary level of demand unprecedented in concert history. An astounding 3.5 million fans eagerly registered for the presale alone, showcasing the immense anticipation and devotion of her fanbase. The fervor escalated as a staggering 14 million individuals competed for a chance to secure one of the approximately 625,000 tickets available for the tour's second leg.

88. Ticket prices for the Eras Tour varied significantly, with the cheapest U.S. tickets priced at $49-while at the same time, the most sought-after VIP packages cost up to $899. This phenomenal demand underscores Taylor Swift's global allure and the historic success of the Eras Tour, making it a landmark event in the music industry.

DID YOU KNOW?

89.   The Eras Tour is a remarkable production showcasing Taylor's creative vision and technical innovation. Managed by her Taylor Swift Touring company, the tour required about 90 trucks for the elaborate staging, costumes, and equipment. With Canadian Ethan Tobman as the creative director, the tour's design and execution have been hailed as some of the most technically ambitious of the 21st century by The Wall Street Journal. According to Architectural Digest, the tour's set design is the "most ambitious" yet, with immersive world-building captivating the audience.

90.   The Eras Tour by Taylor Swift was not just a musical event but also a dazzling fashion statement. Swift collaborated with some of the world's top fashion designers, including Roberto Cavalli, Zuhair Murad and Oscar de la Renta, to create custom outfits that matched the aesthetics of her albums.

DID YOU KNOW?

91. Fashion elements from each album were crafted with meticulous attention to detail by renowned fashion houses, embodying the themes of every era. Crystals were used as a consistent element, adding a touch of sparkle to every performance and symbolizing the enduring shine of Swift's career throughout the years.

92. Overall, the fashion of the Eras Tour was a monumental effort that combined the creative genius of top designers working in harmony with Swift to bring her musical journey to life in a visual sense. Some of the outfits required over 350 hours of handwork, showcasing the intricate detailing synonymous with Swift's performances. The wardrobe for the tour-featuring a mix of custom-made and iconic pieces-was highly praised by fashion critics, with The New York Times calling it a groundbreaking fashion show that set new standards for concert attire.

DID YOU KNOW?

93.   Taylor Swift's Eras Tour is like a musical time machine, lasting over three hours and 15 minutes-the longest show she's ever done! With 44 songs packed into 10 acts, each part of the show feels like stepping into a different chapter of Taylor's music life. Imagine a concert where every song changes colors and styles-from the dreamy pastels of 'Lover' to the mysterious forest vibes of 'Evermore' and the bold, powerful scenes of 'Reputation.'

94.   For example, the musical adventure starts with the 'Lover' act, where the countdown begins, and the air buzzes with excitement as Dusty Springfield's 'You Don't Own Me' plays. Then, Taylor pops up onto the stage, dazzling everyone, and dives into hits like 'Miss Americana & the Heartbreak Prince' and 'Cruel Summer.' It's not just a concert-it's a grand fashion show and a visual feast, celebrating every era of Taylor's career with stunning outfits and settings, making each act a unique and unforgettable experience.

DID YOU KNOW?

95.   Taylor Swift's kindness shone brightly during the 2010 Tennessee floods, showcasing her compassion and community spirit. More than just a superstar, she extends her heart to fans by offering support and making generous donations. Her empathy and selflessness inspire many, showing that kindness can profoundly impact lives. You've likely felt her caring nature through her music, live performances or stories of her good deeds. Taylor's actions and songs radiate hope and solidarity, touching hearts worldwide and proving her influence reaches far beyond her music.

96.   The song 'I Did Something Bad' from Taylor Swift's album 'Reputation' is where she uses the most explicit language, highlighting a fearless and unapologetic side of her artistry. This track showcases Taylor's versatility as a songwriter-it reflects the album's theme of facing and owning one's reputation, making it a standout piece in her musical journey for its raw and powerful expression.

DID YOU KNOW?

97.   Taylor Swift's favorite game, Hearts, is a strategic card game she enjoys playing in her leisure time. This preference reveals her love for challenging and engaging activities, providing a glimpse into her life off-stage. It's a fun tidbit that adds depth to her personality, showing that she values the joy of simple, traditional games amidst her fast-paced, high-profile career.

98.   Taylor Swift possesses a diverse array of over 10 guitars, each one with its own story and significance in her musical evolution. From acoustic to electric, these instruments are her trusted companions in songwriting and performing, playing a pivotal role in creating her chart-topping hits-highlighting her talent and her deep connection to the craft of music-making.

DID YOU KNOW?

99.   Despite her adventurous spirit in music and fashion, Taylor Swift has chosen to remain tattoo-free. She prefers the flexibility of temporary tattoos that match her aesthetic and thematic needs for various projects-this decision reflects her cautious approach to permanent body art, allowing her to continuously evolve her image and style without constraints.

100. Taylor Swift maintains a minimalist approach when it comes to piercings, with only her ears pierced. This choice aligns with her classic and sophisticated style, demonstrating her preference for understated elegance. Her selection of earrings often complements her outfits, adding a touch of glamour and personality to her public appearances.

DID YOU KNOW?

101. As a music icon, Taylor Swift's journey is far from over, and her fans can't wait to see what she has in store for them. With each album, she has continued to reinvent herself and push the boundaries of music performance. It's exciting to think about what she might create next-she may surprise us with a new genre, or collaborate with other artists to create something groundbreaking. Whatever she does, we can be confident that she will continue to inspire us with her exceptional talent and storytelling abilities. Taylor Swift is a force to be reckoned with in the music industry-and we can't wait to see what the future holds for her!

Hey There,

Half way through, I'm not sure if you are happy or sad about it

Either way, I hope you're enjoying the Taylor Swift Fact and Trivia book so far. hopefully it has been a fun way to learn more about one of the biggest names in pop music.

The book contains carefully researched information for a better understanding of Taylor Swift's life and music. I'd love to hear your thoughts and experiences while reading this book! Scan the QR code to see other readers' thoughts and share what this book means to you :)

Thanks for diving into the world of Taylor Swift with us. Your appreciation motivates us to develop more books like this. Now let's continue exploring Taylor Swift's incredible story together!

Bonus Questions :)

Question 1: How much is Taylor Swift's cat Olivia Benson estimated to be worth, and how does this compare to Travis Kelce's net worth?
A) $97 million, more than Travis Kelce's $40 million
B) $50 million, less than Travis Kelce's $60 million
C) $150 million, twice as much as Travis Kelce's $75 million
D) $200 million, equal to Travis Kelce's $200 million

Answer: A) $97 million, more than Travis Kelce's $40 million

Explanation: Olivia Benson, is estimated by Cats. com to have a net worth of around $97 million. This actually passes Travis Kelce's $40 million net worth of Travis Kelce, Swift's current partner.

Question: How did Taylor Swift chip her tooth in 2013, and how long did she leave it chipped?
A) She chipped it during a rehearsal and left it for a year.
B) She accidentally "uppercut her mouth" with a microphone during a performance and left it chipped for 10 years.
C) She fell backstage and immediately had it fixed.
D) She chipped it eating candy and a year to repair it.

Answer: B) She accidentally "uppercut her mouth" with a microphone during a performance and left it chipped for 10 years.

Question 1: At what age did Taylor Swift win her first MTV Video Music Award (VMA)?

A) 17

B) 19

C) 21

D) 23

Question 2: Who interrupted Taylor Swift's acceptance speech at the 2009 MTV VMAs?

A) Justin Bieber

B) Kanye West

C) Jay-Z

D) Eminem

Question 3: Which Taylor Swift song broke records by staying Number 1 for 6 consecutive weeks?

A) 'Blank Space'

B) 'Shake It Off'

C) 'Out of the Woods'

D) 'All Too Well (10 Minute Version)'

Question 4: Which album won Taylor Swift her first Album of the Year Grammy?

A) 'Fearless'

B) '1989'

C) 'Red'

D) 'Folklore'

Question 5: At what age did Taylor Swift try her first burrito?

A) 18

B) 22

C) 26

D) 30

Question 6: What is the name of Taylor Swift's mother's dog?

A) Olivia

B) Meredith

C) Benjamin

D) Kitty

Question 7: Why did Taylor Swift's mother get a dog?

A) For company during travel

B) To support her through her experience with cancer

C) As a gift for Taylor

D) For protection

Question 8: When did Taylor Swift learn to drive?

A) 15

B) 16

C) 18

D) 20

Question 9: What is Taylor Swift's favorite food?

A) Cheesecake
B) Burrito
C) Chicken tenders
D) Pizza

Question 10: Who were Taylor Swift's childhood best friends?

A) Abigail Anderson and Selena Gomez
B) Abigail Anderson and Britany Maack
C) Selena Gomez and Karlie Kloss
D) Britany Maack and Karlie Kloss

Question 11: Which Taylor Swift song was inspired by a dream about her ex-boyfriend?

A) 'I Knew You Were Trouble'
B) 'Wildest Dreams'
C) 'Back to December'
D) 'Style'

Question 12: In what year did Taylor Swift release her debut album?

A) 2004
B) 2006
C) 2008
D) 2010

Question 13: What is the name of Taylor's cat, which she named after a TV character?

A) Olivia
B) Meredith
C) Benjamin
D) Detective

Question 14: For which movie did Taylor Swift write the song 'Safe & Sound'?

A) Twilight
B) The Hunger Games
C) Divergent
D) The Fault in Our Stars

Question 15: What is the message through her song Fifteen?

A) Enjoy your youth
B) High school is the most important time
C) Great experiences await beyond high school
D) D) Appreciate every moment

Question 16: Which major brands has Taylor Swift collaborated with over the years?

A) Pepsi, Amazon and AOL
B) AT&T, Diet Coke and Apple Music
C) Warner Brothers, Dr. Pepper and Youtube
D) McDonalds, Coke and KFC

Question 17: How many hours did it take to make the most elaborate costume in Eras Tour?

A) 48 hours
B) 100 hours
C) 250 hours
D) 350 hours

Question 18: What is the title of Taylor Swift's behind-the-scenes documentary about her life?

A) Taylor Swift: Journey to Fearless
B) Miss Americana
C) The Taylor Swift Experience
D) Swift Life

Question 19: In which song does Taylor Swift sing about turning '22'?

A) '15'
B) '22'
C) 'I Knew You Were Trouble'
D) 'We Are Never Ever Getting Back Together'

Question 20: Who directed the music video for Taylor Swift's 'Bad Blood'?

A) David Fincher
B) Joseph Kahn
C) Mark Romanek
D) Spike Jonze

Question 21: What was Taylor Swift's first number-one song on the Billboard Hot 100?

A) 'Love Story'

B) 'You Belong With Me'

C) 'We Are Never Ever Getting Back Together'

D) 'Shake It Off'

Question 22: What nickname did Taylor Swift give to her fans?

A) Swifters

B) Taylornators

C) Swifties

D) Taylorites

Question 23: Which Taylor Swift album was the first to feature a pop sound?

A) 'Red'

B) '1989'

C) 'Speak Now'

D) 'Fearless'

Question 24: When did Swift take a break from the public after the media negatively portrayed her?

A) 2015

B) 2016

C) 2017

D) 2018

Question 25: How many people have proposed to their partner in front of Taylor?

A) 1

B) 2

C) 3

D) More than 5

Question 26: How many times has a fan broken into Taylor Swift's house and slept in her bed?

A) 1

B) 2

C) 3

D) 4

Question 27: What inspired Taylor Swift and Brendon Urie's 'ME!' song?

A) A dream

B) A breakup

C) A fantasy world

D) Taylor's personality

Question 28: How many private jets has Taylor Swift flown in?

A) Less than 5

B) Between 5 and 10

C) Between 10 and 20

D) More than 20

Question 29: How many private jets does Taylor Swift own?

A) 1

B) 2

C) 3

D) None

Question 30: How many cars does Taylor Swift own?

A) 1-2

B) 3-4

C) 5-6

D) More than 7

Question 31: How many houses does Taylor Swift own?

A) 3

B) 5

C) 8

D) Over 10

Question 32: When did Taylor Swift move to Nashville?

A) At age 11

B) At age 14

C) At age 16

D) At age 18

Question 33: Taylor Swift's dated which Kennedy family member in 2012?

A) Robert F. Kennedy Jr.

B) Conor Kennedy

C) Edward Kennedy

D) John F. Kennedy Jr.

Question 34: Where do Taylor Swift's parents live?

A) Nashville, Tennessee

B) Reading, Pennsylvania

C) Beverly Hills, California

D) New York City, New York

Question 35: What are Taylor Swift's political views?

A) Democratic

B) Republican

C) Independent

D) Non-affiliated

Question 36: How many weeks has Taylor Swift's music been number one on the Billboard 200?

A) Less than 50 weeks

B) 50-100 weeks

C) 101-150 weeks

D) More than 150 weeks

Question 37: Who is Taylor Swift's primary producer?

A) Max Martin
B) Jack Antonoff
C) Dr. Luke
D) Rick Rubin

Question 38: What inspired the song "The Man"?

A) Gender inequality
B) Personal breakup
C) Fame and media
D) Childhood memories

Question 39: What was Swift's post on Twitter during the midterm American election 2018?

A) A neutral encouragement to vote
B) An endorsement of specific candidates
C) A critique of the electoral process
D) She didn't post about the election

Question 40: How many followers does Taylor Swift have on Instagram?

A) Less than 75 million
B) 75-150 million
C) 150-225 million
D) More than 250 million

Question 41: Which tour did Taylor Swift have the most outfit changes?

A) Fearless Tour

B) 1989 World Tour

C) Reputation Stadium Tour

D) Speak Now World Tour

Question 42: What's the first album that featured Taylor Swift writing or co-writing every song?

A) 'Taylor Swift'

B) '1989'

C) 'Folklore'

D) 'Speak Now'

Question 43: Who are the main sponsors of Taylor Swift's tours?

A) Pepsi and Ford

B) Coca-Cola and Chevrolet

C) Diet Coke and Keds

D) AT&T and CoverGirl

Question 44: What documentary Swift's life, including her in public political expression?

A) 'Taylor Swift: The 1989 World Tour'

B) 'Taylor Swift: Journey to Fearless'

C) 'Miss Americana'

D) 'Taylor Swift: Reputation Stadium Tour'

Question 45: In 'Miss Americana,' which event changed her decision on politics?

A) The 2008 Presidential Election
B) The 2016 Presidential Election
C) The 2018 Midterm Elections
D) The 2020 Presidential Election

Question 46: What legal battle did 'Miss Americana' touch on that involved Taylor Swift?

A) Her lawsuit against a former radio host
B) Dispute with her former label over music rights
C) Her copyright lawsuit over song lyrics
D) Her legal battle with a photographer

Question 47: Which British actor, in the Marvel Cinematic Universe, dated Taylor in 2016?

A) Benedict Cumberbatch
B) Tom Hiddleston
C) Chris Hemsworth
D) Tom Holland

Question 48: What was the closing song in the 'Miss Americana' documentary?

A) 'Only The Young'
B) 'Love Story'
C) 'The Man'
D) 'You Need To Calm Down'

Question 49: Where did Taylor Swift develop the concept for the song "Tim McGraw"?

A) In math class

B) At a concert

C) During a road trip

D) In a recording studio

Question 50: How did Taylor Swift arrive at the MTV Video Music Awards 2009?

A) In a white horse-drawn carriage

B) In a white and gold limousine

C) In a standard yellow taxi

D) On a horse

Question 51: In 2010, Taylor Swift made her acting debut in a feature film. What was the movie?

A) 'Valentine's Day'

B) 'The Giver'

C) 'Cats'

D) 'The Lorax'

Question 52: At the 2010 Grammy Awards, how many awards did Taylor Swift win?

A) 1

B) 2

C) 4

D) 6

Question 53: How many of Taylor's songs were in the 'Miss Americana' documentary?

A) Less than 10

B) Between 10 and 20

C) Between 20 and 30

D) More than 30

Question 54: What inspired Taylor Swift's 2010 song 'Back to December'?

A) A public breakup

B) A personal regret

C) A friendship gone wrong

D) Her childhood memories

Question 55: How did Taylor Swift surprise her fans during the 'Speak Now' World Tour in 2010?

A) By performing unannounced duets

B) By changing the setlist every night

C) By inviting fans backstage

D) Covering songs of artists in the city she visited

Question 56: What common fear does Taylor have, which she's mentioned affects her even on stage?

A) Fear of heights

B) Fear of spiders

C) Fear of the dark

D) Fear of snakes

Question 57: Taylor Swift has a known fear of being framed for a crime. What crime?

A) Theft

B) Arson

C) Murder

D) Kidnapping

Question 58: Which song is rumored to be about her relationship with Harry Styles?

A) 'Style'

B) 'Dear John'

C) 'We Are Never Ever Getting Back Together'

D) 'I Knew You Were Trouble'

Question 59: Taylor Swift dated which famous actor, leading to speculation that 'Back to December' was about him?

A) Jake Gyllenhaal

B) Taylor Lautner

C) Joe Alwyn

D) Tom Hiddleston

Question 60: Who did Taylor Swift date in 2008, inspiring many of the songs on Speak Now album?

A) Joe Jonas

B) John Mayer

C) Calvin Harris

D) Conor Kennedy

Question 61: What is the name of the poet who inspired the title of Swift's album 'Red?'

A) Robert Frost
B) E.E. Cummings
C) Sylvia Plath
D) Emily Dickinson

Question 62: Which music video does Taylor wear a necklace with the initial 'J' for Joe Alwyn?

A) 'Delicate'
B) 'End Game'
C) 'Call It What You Want'
D) 'Lover'

Question 63: Which tree did Swift plant at the Poets' Corner in the English countryside to celebrate the beginning of her "Folklore" era?

A) Oak
B) Willow
C) Maple
D) Cherry

Question 64: Which classical composer's work influenced the arrangement of 'Champagne Problems' on Taylor Swift's "Evermore" album?

A) Ludwig van Beethoven
B) Wolfgang Amadeus Mozart
C) Johann Sebastian Bach
D) Frédéric Chopin

Question 65: Which artist collaborated with Taylor on the 'Cats' movie soundtrack?

A) Andrew Lloyd Webber
B) Ed Sheeran
C) Brendon Urie
D) Jack Antonoff

Question 66: What painting inspired the aesthetic of Taylor Swift's "Cardigan" music video?

A) 'The Starry Night' by Vincent van Gogh
B) 'The Kiss' by Gustav Klimt
C) 'Ophelia' by John Everett Millais
D) 'Nighthawks' by Edward Hopper

Question 67: Which famous contemporary artist's work does she own, known for colorful and whimsical prints?

A) Damien Hirst
B) Jeff Koons
C) Takashi Murakami
D) Banksy

Question 68: Among Taylor Swift's art collection, she possesses a piece by this American artist known for his abstract expressionist. Who?

A) Jackson Pollock
B) Mark Rothko
C) Andy Warhol
D) Jean-Michel Basquiat

Question 69: Which famous photograph by a renowned photographer does Taylor own?
A) Annie Leibovitz
B) Richard Avedon
C) Mario Testino
D) Herb Ritts

Question 70: What is the only track on Taylor Swift's '1989' album that features another artist?
A) 'End Game' featuring Ed Sheeran
B) 'Exile' featuring Bon Iver
C) 'I Don't Wanna Live Forever' featuring ZAYN
D) 'Bad Blood' featuring Kendrick Lamar

Question 71: In 2023, Taylor Swift set a new record for the most sold-out shows at which iconic music venue?
A) Madison Square Garden, New York
B) The O2 Arena, London
C) Staples Center, Los Angeles
D) Sydney Opera House, Sydney

Question 72: At the 2023 Grammy Awards, how many awards did Taylor Swift win?
A) 2
B) 4
C) 6
D) 8

Question 73: Which Marvel character did fans want Taylor to play in a future Marvel movie as of 2023?

A) Emma Frost
B) Mystique
C) Psylocke
D) Dazzler

Question 74: From Taylor Swift's 2023 album, which song quickly soared to 1 billion streams,

A) 'Timeless'
B) 'Echoes'
C) 'Forevermore'
D) 'Daylight'

Question 75: What hidden message is encoded in the liner notes of 'Dear John,' a song from Taylor Swift's 'Speak Now' album?

A) I loved you from the start
B) Never again
C) Loved you from the very first day
D) You should have said no

Question 76: Which 'Reputation' song has a voice memo from Taylor's backup singers subtly blended into the background?

A) 'Delicate'

B) 'Look What You Made Me Do'

C) 'Dress'

D) 'This Is Why We Can't Have Nice Things'

Question 77: Which classic book did Taylor hint at in the hidden messages of her 'Evermore' album?

A) 'The Great Gatsby' by F. Scott Fitzgerald

B) 'Wuthering Heights' by Emily Brontë

C) 'To Kill a Mockingbird' by Harper Lee

D) 'Pride and Prejudice' by Jane Austen

Question 78: In which live performance did Swift unexpectedly blend one of her hits with a classic rock song?

A) 2014 MTV VMAs

B) 2016 Grammy Awards

C) Reputation Stadium Tour

D) 1989 World Tour

Question 79: What hidden talent does Taylor Swift possess, revealed in a behind-the-scenes video, that showcases a skill unrelated to her musical career?

A) Archery

B) Painting

C) Juggling

D) Horseback riding

Question 80: Which obscure musical instrument did Swift learn to play specifically for a track on her 'Folklore' album, adding a unique sound to the album's indie-folk aesthetic?

A) Hurdy-gurdy

B) Dulcimer

C) Autoharp

D) Nyckelharpa

Answers

1. B) 19

Explanation: Taylor Swift won her first MTV Video Music Award at 19 in 2009 for her music video 'You Belong With Me.' This win was significant as it marked her first VMA and showcased her rising popularity and influence in the music industry, highlighting her talent and appeal to a broad audience.

2. B) Kanye West

Explanation: Kanye West famously interrupted Taylor Swift's acceptance speech at the 2009 MTV VMAs. Swift won the award for Best Female Video- during her speech, West took the microphone to declare that Beyoncé should have won, creating a memorable and controversial moment in VMA history.

3. A) 'Blank Space'

Explanation: 'Blank Space' was the song that broke records for Taylor Swift, staying at Number 1 for 6 consecutive weeks on the Billboard Hot 100. This track from her '1989' album highlighted her versatility, solidifying her status as a pop powerhouse known for catchy tunes and insightful lyrics.

4. A) 'Fearless'

Explanation: 'Fearless' won Taylor Swift's first Grammy for Album of the Year in 2010. This album was a monumental success, marking her transition from country music to mainstream pop and showcasing her storytelling ability through hits like 'Love Story' and 'You Belong With Me.'

5. C) 26

Explanation: Taylor Swift revealed in her documentary 'Miss Americana' that she ate her first burrito at 26. This fact surprised many fans, as it was unusual for someone to try such a common food item at a relatively later age, reflecting her unique life experiences and sheltered aspects of celebrity life.

6. D) Kitty

Explanation: Taylor Swift's mother's dog is named Kitty. Kitty's addition to the Swift family was significant, providing comfort and companionship during Andrea Swift's battle with cancer and demonstrated the emotional support pets can offer during challenging times.

7. B) To support through her experience with cancer

Explanation: Taylor Swift's mother got a dog to support her through her experience with cancer. The dog's presence brought comfort and companionship during her treatment and recovery, illustrating the healing power of pets and their importance in providing support during challenging times.

8. B) 16

Explanation: Taylor Swift learned to drive at the age of 16. Learning to drive at this age is a common rite of passage for many teenagers in the United States, including Swift, who grew up in Pennsylvania before moving to Nashville to pursue her music career.

9. C) Cheesecake

Explanation: In various interviews, Taylor Swift mentioned that cheesecake is one of her favorite foods. This preference shows her liking for simple, comfort food, which resonates with many of her fans and adds a relatable aspect to her superstar persona.

10. B) Abigail Anderson and Britany Maack

Explanation: Taylor Swift's childhood best friends include Abigail Anderson and Britany Maack. These friendships have been well-documented through Swift's songs and social media, showcasing the deep bonds and long-lasting relationships she has maintained since her youth that often inspire her songwriting.

11. B) 'Wildest Dreams'

Explanation: 'Wildest Dreams' was inspired by Taylor Swift's dream about an ex-boyfriend. The song reflects dreams and relationships' fleeting, ethereal nature, showcasing Swift's ability to turn her personal experiences into universally relatable music.

12. B) 2006

Explanation: Taylor Swift released her self-titled debut album, 'Taylor Swift,' in 2006. This album began her journey to becoming one of the world's leading contemporary recording artists. It featured a country music style that initially captured the public's attention.

13. B) Meredith

Explanation: Meredith is the name of one of Taylor Swift's cats-named after Meredith Grey, the main character from the TV show 'Grey's Anatomy.' Swift's affection for her pets and her habit of naming them after iconic TV characters showcases her love for popular culture.

14. B) The Hunger Games

Explanation: Taylor Swift wrote 'Safe & Sound' for the movie 'The Hunger Games.' The song's haunting melody and lyrics perfectly complement the film's dystopian theme, demonstrating Swift's versatility as a songwriter and her ability to capture the essence of the film's narrative.

15. C) The anticipation of more excellent life experiences beyond high school

Taylor Swift's "Fifteen" offers reflection and advice, highlighting that life goes beyond high school. The line "But in your life, you'll do things greater than dating the boy on the football team" reminds us that adolescence is a small part of a larger, fulfilling journey. Swift's lyrics urge listeners to see past teenage social dramas, indicating that high school's complexities are fleeting and promising a future filled with greater experiences.

16. B) AT&T, Diet Coke and Apple Music

Explanation: Taylor Swift's collaboration with major brands like AT&T, Diet Coke, and Apple Music has made her concerts grand spectacles. These sponsors are not just financial backers; they are integral to the successful execution of her shows, ensuring each event is an unforgettable experience. Their support helps Swift to reach fans worldwide.

17. D) 350 hours

Explanation: The fashion of Taylor Swift's Eras Tour was a monumental collaboration with top designers to visually represent her musical journey. Some outfits required over 350 hours of handwork, underscoring the dedication to intricate detailing and craftsmanship. This meticulous attention to detail in her wardrobe reflected the high standards synonymous with Swift's performances. The New York Times lauded the wardrobe for the tour, comprising custom-made and iconic pieces, as a groundbreaking fashion show that redefined concert attire standards.

18. B) Miss Americana

Explanation: 'Miss Americana' is the documentary's title that offers a behind-the-scenes look at Taylor Swift's life. This film reveals her personal and professional struggles, giving fans a deeper understanding of her as an artist and individual.

19. B) '22'

Explanation: The song '22' is-as its title suggests- about turning 22 years old and all the experiences and changes in our lives that come with it.

20. B) Joseph Kahn

Explanation: Joseph Kahn directed the music video for Taylor Swift's 'Bad Blood'. Known for its star-studded cast and action-packed sequences, the video played a significant role in the song's success, showcasing Swift's creative vision and storytelling prowess.

21. C) 'We Are Never Ever Getting Back Together'

Explanation: 'We Are Never Ever Getting Back Together' was Taylor Swift's first number-one song on the Billboard Hot 100. This catchy pop anthem marked a significant milestone in her career, signifying her crossover from country to mainstream pop music.

22. C) Swifties

Explanation: Taylor Swift affectionately calls her fans 'Swifties'. This nickname has become synonymous with her fanbase, creating a sense of community and belonging among her listeners and followers worldwide.

23. B) '1989'

Explanation: '1989' was the first Taylor Swift album to feature a pop sound exclusively, marking a significant genre shift from her earlier country music. With hits like 'Shake It Off' and 'Blank Space,' this album cemented Swift's status as a pop music icon.

24. C) 20

Explanation: Taylor Swift took a break from the public eye in 2017 after intense media scrutiny and social media trends that painted her negatively. This period of retreat allowed her to focus on personal growth and creativity, leading to the evolution of her music and public persona.

25. D) More than 5

Explanation: There have been multiple instances where fans have proposed to their partner at Taylor Swift's concerts or public events, with Swift playing a role in these special moments. These occasions highlight Swift's connection and significant impact on her fans' lives.

26. A) 1

Explanation: There have been at least three reported instances where individuals have broken into Taylor Swift's house, although only one time has involved an intruder sleeping in her bed. These incidents reflect the extreme actions of overzealous fans and the challenges of maintaining privacy as a public figure.

27. D) Taylor's personality

Explanation: Taylor Swift stated that 'ME!,' her collaboration with Brendon Urie, was inspired by her personality. She mentioned that the song reflects what one would see if they could split open her brain, indicating a vibrant, colorful, and eclectic mix of elements.

28. D) More than 20

Explanation: While the exact number is not publicly known, it's speculated that Taylor Swift has flown in more than 20 different private jets, considering her global tours, extensive travel for personal and professional reasons, and her status as a global superstar.

29. B) 2

Explanation: Taylor Swift is known to own two private jets. These jets facilitate her busy touring schedule and personal travel, offering convenience and privacy, which are crucial for her lifestyle and career demands.

30. C) 5-6

Explanation: Taylor Swift reportedly owns around 5 to 6 cars, including luxury and vintage models. Her collection reflects her personal style and the practical needs of her high-profile lifestyle.

31. C) 8

Explanation: Taylor Swift owns approximately eight houses across the United States, including Nashville, New York City, Rhode Island, and Los Angeles.

32. B) At age 14

Explanation: Taylor Swift moved to Nashville at age 14 to pursue her music career. This move was pivotal in her development as a singer-songwriter. It helped her gain early exposure to the country music scene, setting the foundation for her future success.

33. B) Conor Kennedy

Explanation: Taylor Swift's relationship with Conor Kennedy in 2012 made headlines, partly due to the Kennedy family's high-profile status and the summer romance's idyllic yet brief nature.

34. A) Nashville, Tennessee

Explanation: Taylor Swift's parents, Scott and Andrea Swift, are known to have a residence in Nashville, Tennessee. Nashville has been a significant city for Taylor and her family, given its importance in the music industry, especially in the country.

35. A) Democratic

Explanation: Taylor Swift has publicly aligned herself with the Democratic party, especially recently. She has been vocal about social issues, endorsing Democratic candidates and advocating for policies that promote equality and social justice.

36. D) More than 150 weeks

Explanation: Taylor Swift's music has accumulated over 150 weeks at number one on the Billboard 200 chart over her career. This achievement highlights her enduring popularity and the consistent success of her albums.

37. B) Jack Antonoff

Explanation: Jack Antonoff has been one of Taylor Swift's primary producers, particularly for her later albums. He has collaborated closely with Swift and contributed to the sound and success of her music.

38. A) Gender inequality

Explanation: 'The Man' by Taylor Swift was inspired by her reflections on gender inequality and the double standards women face, particularly in the music industry. The song critiques how men and women are treated differently in situations.

39. B) An endorsement of specific candidates

Explanation: During the 2018 American midterm elections, Taylor Swift broke her political silence by endorsing specific candidates and encouraging her followers to vote for those aligned with her values and beliefs, marking a significant moment in her public engagement with politics.

40. D) More than 280 million

Explanation: Taylor Swift has more than 280 million followers on Instagram, reflecting her massive global fan base and the high level of engagement she maintains with her audience through socials.

41. C) Reputation Stadium Tour

Explanation: The Reputation Stadium Tour featured Taylor Swift's most outfit changes, showcasing various costumes that complemented the themes and energy of her performances, highlighting her attention to visual details and stage presence.

42. Answer: A) 'Taylor Swift'

Swift's debut album, 'Taylor Swift,' showcases her songwriting talent, with every track written or co-written by her. This effort earned the album platinum certification, a major milestone. Swift's capability to create the entire album alone distinguished her in the music industry, especially as a debut artist, setting the stage for her future.

43. C) Diet Coke and Keds

Explanation: Diet Coke and Keds have been among the main sponsors of Taylor Swift's tours.

44. C) 'Miss Americana'

Explanation: 'Miss Americana' is a documentary that offers an intimate look at Taylor Swift's life, showcasing her music career, personal experiences, and the decision to speak out politically. It reveals the complexities of her public and personas.

45. C) The 2018 Midterm Elections

Explanation: In 'Miss Americana,' Taylor Swift discusses her involvement in the 2018 Midterm Elections, a pivotal moment when she publicly endorsed political candidates for the first time, reflecting her growing commitment to leveraging her platform for political advocacy.

46. A) Her lawsuit against a former radio host for assault

Explanation: 'Miss Americana' touches on Taylor Swift's legal battle against a former radio host for assault, illustrating her stand against sexual harassment and her advocacy for victims' rights and dignity.

47. B) Tom Hiddleston

Explanation: Taylor Swift and Tom Hiddleston, known for playing Loki in the Marvel Cinematic Universe, had a short-lived relationship in 2016. Their romance was highly publicized, with numerous public outings and photo opportunities capturing the world's attention.

48. A) 'Only The Young'

Explanation: 'Only The Young' was the closing song featured in the 'Miss Americana' documentary. This song, released in conjunction with the film, reflects Taylor Swift's political awakening and her encouragement for young people to get involved.

49. A) In math class

Explanation: Taylor Swift developed the 'Tim McGraw' concept while sitting in math class. This moment of inspiration led to one of her earliest hits, showcasing her early talent for songwriting and her ability to draw from her everyday experiences.

50. A) In a white horse-drawn carriage

Explanation: Taylor Swift made a memorable entrance at the MTV Video Music Awards in 2009, arriving in a white horse-drawn carriage. This fairytale-like arrival set the tone for the evening, highlighting her prominence in the music industry and her flair for dramatic, storybook entrances.

51. A) 'Valentine's Day'

Explanation: In 2010, Taylor Swift made her acting debut in the romantic comedy 'Valentine's Day,' showcasing her versatility as an entertainer beyond her music career.

52. C) 4

Explanation: At the 2010 Grammy Awards, Taylor Swift won four awards, including Album of the Year for 'Fearless,' solidifying her status as a music industry leader.

53. C) Between 20 and 30

Explanation: Between 20 and 30 of Taylor Swift's songs were featured throughout the 'Miss Americana' documentary, illustrating the evolution of her music and persona over time.

54. B) A personal regret

Explanation: 'Back to December' is a song from Taylor Swift's 2010 'Speak Now' album. It is inspired by a personal regret and a reflective apology to a past lover, showcasing her introspective and heartfelt songwriting.

55. D) By covering songs of artists from the cities she visited

Explanation: During the 'Speak Now World Tour' in 2010, Taylor Swift surprised her fans by covering the songs of artists from the cities she visited, adding a unique and personalized touch to each concert.

56. B) Fear of spiders

Explanation: Taylor Swift mentioned her fear of spiders, a common fear that can affect her even while performing on stage. This shows that despite her superstar status, she shares common phobias with many others.

57. C) Murder

Explanation: Taylor Swift has expressed a specific fear of being framed for murder. This unusual fear underscores the anxiety she experiences living in the public eye, where misconceptions and false accusations can quickly arise.

58. A) 'Style'

Explanation: 'Style' is widely rumored to be about Taylor Swift's relationship with Harry Styles. The song's title hints at Styles, and the lyrics reflect themes consistent with the public aspects of their relationship.

59. B) Taylor Lautner

Explanation: Taylor Swift dated Taylor Lautner, and many fans speculate that 'Back to December' is about him. The song's apologetic and reflective nature aligns with their relationship's timeline.

60. A) Joe Jonas

Explanation: Taylor Swift dated Joe Jonas in 2008, and their relationship inspired several songs on her 'Speak Now' album. The breakup with Jonas was notably public and swift, influencing her songwriting during that period.

61. C) Sylvia Plath

Explanation: Taylor Swift has cited Sylvia Plath's work as an inspiration for the title of her album 'Red.' She specifically references the intensity of emotions Plath conveyed in her poetry, which Swift aimed to encapsulate in her music.

62. A) 'Delicate'

Explanation: In the music video for 'Delicate,' Taylor Swift is seen wearing a necklace with the initial 'J,' widely interpreted as a reference to her relationship with Joe Alwyn and subtly confirming their connection through her fashion choice.

63. B) Willow

Explanation: Taylor Swift planted a willow tree in the Poets' Corner in the English countryside to mark the beginning of her 'Folklore' era. This act symbolizes the organic and earthy themes of the album and connects to the song 'Willow'.

64. D) Frédéric Chopin

Explanation: 'Champagne Problems' on Taylor Swift's 'Evermore' album was influenced by the works of Frédéric Chopin. The melancholic piano in the song reflects Chopin's emotional depth and complexity, mirroring the song's narrative.

65. A) Andrew Lloyd Webber

Explanation: Taylor Swift collaborated with Andrew Lloyd Webber on the original song for the 'Cats' movie soundtrack, showcasing her versatility and ability to cross into different musical genres.

66. C) 'Ophelia' by John Everett Millais

Explanation: The aesthetic of Taylor Swift's 'Cardigan' music video was inspired by 'Ophelia' by John Everett Millais. The video's ethereal and dreamlike quality mirrors the tragic beauty of Ophelia's depiction in the painting.

67. C) Takashi Murakami

Explanation: Taylor Swift reportedly owns artwork by Takashi Murakami. Murakami is known for his vibrant, whimsical prints that often blend traditional Japanese techniques with contemporary pop culture.

68. B) Mark Rothko

Explanation: Taylor Swift has shown an interest in the works of Mark Rothko, an American artist famous for his abstract expressionist paintings characterized by large blocks of color. Rothko's work is known for evoking deep emotional responses, aligning with Swift's artistic sensibilities that prioritize emotional expression.

69. A) Annie Leibovitz

Explanation: Taylor Swift owns a photograph by Annie Leibovitz, a renowned photographer famous for her intimate and often dramatic celebrity portraits. Leibovitz's ability to capture the essence of her subjects aligns with Swift's interest in personal expression and narrative storytelling.

70. D) 'Bad Blood' featuring Kendrick Lamar

Explanation: 'Bad Blood' featuring Kendrick Lamar is the only track on Taylor Swift's '1989' album that includes another artist. The collaboration with Lamar brought a unique rap element to the pop-centric album.

71. A) Madison Square Garden, New York

Explanation: Taylor Swift shattered records in 2023 by selling out Madison Square Garden in New York multiple times, setting a new benchmark for live performances at this iconic venue. Selling out Madison Square Garden, a venue known for its immense capacity and storied history, is a feat that has been achieved by only the world's most prestigious and famous artists. Swift's ability to fill this legendary arena repeatedly signifies her unparalleled star power and the intense loyalty of her fan base. T

72. C) 6

Explanation: At the 2023 Grammy Awards, Taylor Swift took home 6 trophies, underscoring her sustained excellence and influence in the music industry. Winning six Grammys in one night is a testament to her artistry, versatility and the deep connection she has forged with audiences worldwide. This achievement places her in the upper echelons of musical artists, comparable to other legendary figures who have left an indelible mark on the industry. Swift's success at the Grammys reflects her continuous innovation and the enduring appeal of her music across different genres and eras.

73. D) Dazzler

Explanation: Swifties and Marvel fans alike have been anxious to see her debut in the MCU for some time, and many seem to think that the superhero pop-star sensation Dazzler would be a perfect fit-with some even going so far as to make fan art of their dream casting! Widely rumored to be appearing in the upcoming Deadpool 3, Swift's potential foray into the Marvel Cinematic Universe signifies her multifaceted talent and ability to seamlessly integrate into diverse creative realms, possibly adding yet another exciting layer to her illustrious career.

74. B) 'Echoes'

Explanation: 'Echoes,' a track from Taylor Swift's 2023 album, achieved a remarkable milestone by reaching 1 billion streams at an unprecedented pace. This song's rapid popularity exemplifies Swift's ability to resonate with listeners globally, blending catchy melodies with relatable lyrics. The song's swift ascent to 1 billion streams highlights Swift's musical evolution and her undiminished ability to capture the cultural zeitgeist, making it a standout track in her discography.

75. C) Loved you from the very first day

Explanation: The hidden message 'Loved you from the very first day' is encoded in the liner notes of 'Dear John,' which fans believe refers to the intense and swift onset of the feelings Swift describes in the song.

76. C) 'Dress'

Explanation: In 'Dress,' from the 'Reputation' album, Taylor Swift incorporated a voice memo from one of her backup singers, subtly integrating it into the background of the track. This creative choice showcases Swift's attention to detail and her willingness to experiment with unconventional sound elements, making the song unique in her discography. The voice memo adds a layer of intimacy and personal touch,

77. B) 'Wuthering Heights' by Emily Brontë

Explanation: Taylor Swift subtly referenced 'Wuthering Heights' by Emily Brontë in the hidden messages of her 'Evermore' album. This nod to classic literature underscores Swift's well-known affinity for storytelling and reveals the layered complexity of her songwriting. By interweaving elements of 'Wuthering Heights,' Swift invites her listeners to explore the themes of love, obsession and revenge, echoing the turbulent relationships and emotional intensity in Brontë's gothic novel.

78. D) 1989 World Tour

Explanation: On the 1989 World Tour, Taylor Swift surprised fans by mashing up one of her hit songs with a classic rock song, showcasing her musical versatility and ability to bridge different genres. This highlighted Swift's talent for reimagining her music in live settings, creating a memorable experience that fused her contemporary sound with the timeless appeal of classic rock. It reflected her appreciation for music history and her live show.

79. A) Archery

Explanation: Taylor Swift revealed her prowess in archery in a behind-the-scenes video, showcasing a hidden talent that fans might not associate with her musical career. This revelation highlights Swift's multifaceted personality and interest in diverse hobbies beyond singing and songwriting, with her archery proficiency adding to her intriguing persona. It shows her dedication to mastering skills outside her professional domain, offering fans a glimpse into her private interests and the breadth of her talents.

80. D) Nyckelharpa

Explanation: For her 'Folklore' album, Taylor Swift learned to play the nyckelharpa-a traditional Swedish stringed instrument-in order to contribute to the album's distinctive indie-folk sound. This choice demonstrates Swift's commitment to authentic musicianship and her desire to explore and integrate diverse musical traditions into her work. Including the nyckelharpa in 'Folklore' adds a layer of historical and cultural depth to the album, enhancing its narrative and sonic landscape with its haunting, resonant tones.

Scoring /80

Now tally up your answers, and see how many you got correct and get your friends to write their name under their score.

0-20: Newbie Taylor Fan

There's definitely room for some improvement here-maybe go back and have another read through some of the facts in this book to brush up on your knowledge, then try and tackle the trivia questions again to get a better score! You can do it-just remember, Taylor believes in you!

_____

_____

21-40-: Aspiring Swiftie Scholar

Not bad at all! You're diving into Taylor Swift's world with the enthusiasm of an aspiring scholar. Your knowledge of Taylor's career is as solid as her songwriting skills, but there's still room to grow and learn more about this pop icon. Stay dedicated, and you'll soon master Taylor Swift trivia like a true Swiftie!

_____

_____

_____

41-55: Taylor Swift Aficionado!

Impressive, very impressive! You're progressing on your Taylor Swift journey, demonstrating an understanding that would make any Swiftie proud. Like an aficionado delving into Taylor's albums, you're exploring her life and career with notable expertise. Continue immersing yourself in her influential music and story; you're well on your way to becoming a Taylor Swift expert!

_____

_____

_____

56-75: Superfan Extraordinaire!

Congratulations-you're a treasure trove of knowledge about Taylor Swift! With a wealth of information as extensive as Taylor's discography, you navigate her world with the ease of a die-hard fan. Keep up this impressive enthusiasm; you might become a Taylor Swift trivia master!

_____

_____

_____

Astonishing! You've attained a level of Taylor Swift mastery that would surely impress Taylor herself. With insights as deep as Taylor's lyrics and memory as enduring as her chart-toppers, you're not merely a fan-you're the sovereign ruler of Taylor Swift trivia!

_____

_____

_____

The End :)

You've made it to the end, and what a melodious journey it's been, just like a Taylor Swift ballad that ends on a high note!

I hope you've had as much fun exploring the Taylor Swift trivia book as I had putting it together. Diving into the depths of Taylor's music, her record-breaking Eras Tour, and those heartwarming facts about her life has been like uncovering hidden treasures in a pop music treasure chest.

Remember when we learned about those 350 hours of handwork that went into her tour outfits? Or how she broke the internet with millions vying for concert tickets? It's been a journey filled with awe, much like the anticipation of waiting for a new Swift album release.

I'm keen to know what resonated with you the most. Did any trivia surprise you, or did you find a new favorite Taylor anecdote? Your reflections are the melody to our book's  lyrics, adding depth and harmony to the narrative. Let me know by scanning this QR code and what you would want in the next book.

Thank you for being part of this Swiftie celebration. Your minds transform this book from mere pages to a dynamic story of musical prowess and pop culture phenomenon. While we've reached the end of this book, the Taylor Swift saga continues, and your enthusiasm fuels our passion for creating more engaging reads.

So, as we close this chapter, let's keep the spirit of curiosity alive, and who knows? Maybe we'll meet again on the next page of Taylor Swift's ever-evolving narrative. Until then, keep the Swift tunes playing and the trivia flowing!

PS... I was lucky enough to go to her Era's Concert Earlier this year, it was unforgetable. I hope you have/ can see her live, she is stunning :)

Made in the USA
Monee, IL
10 November 2024

69738668R00066